W9-BCY-487

# VACCINE WARS:

## When Science and Politics Collide

John Allen

ReferencePoint
Press

San Diego, CA

© 2022 ReferencePoint Press, Inc.
Printed in the United States

**For more information, contact:**
ReferencePoint Press, Inc.
PO Box 27779
San Diego, CA 92198
www.ReferencePointPress.com

LIBRARY OF CONGRESS CATALOGING-IN-PUBLICATION DATA

Names: Allen, John, 1957- author.
Title: Vaccine wars : when science and politics collide / John Allen.
Description: San Diego, CA : ReferencePoint Press, Inc., 2022. | Includes
    bibliographical references and index.
Identifiers: LCCN 2021013184 (print) | LCCN 2021013185 (ebook) | ISBN
    9781678201807 (library binding) | ISBN 9781678201814 (ebook)
Subjects: LCSH: Vaccines--Juvenile literature. | Vaccination--Juvenile
    literature. | Communicable diseases--Prevention--History--Juvenile
    literature.
Classification: LCC RA638 .A46 2022  (print) | LCC RA638  (ebook) | DDC
    615.3/72--dc23
LC record available at https://lccn.loc.gov/2021013184
LC ebook record available at https://lccn.loc.gov/2021013185

# CONTENTS

# Fighting Fear and Skepticism

During a focus group in March 2021, nineteen Republican voters discussed their unease with the new vaccines for COVID-19. The vaccines were created in record time to prevent people from contracting the coronavirus. Although insisting they were not anti-vaccine, the voters admitted to concerns about mixed messages from politicians and government scientists. Some felt that the threat of COVID-19 had been overhyped. Political ads urging them to get vaccinated had only increased their skepticism. Not even former president Donald Trump's endorsement made much difference. As veteran Republican pollster Frank Luntz noted, such widespread views among holdouts could jeopardize the entire vaccine effort. "These people represent 30 million Americans," said Luntz. "And without these people, you're not getting herd immunity."[1] Herd immunity is achieved when a sufficiently large proportion of the populace becomes immune to a disease and the pathogen is no longer able to spread.

Presented with a clear statement of facts about the vaccines, the voters in the focus group all changed their minds and declared their willingness to get the shots. However, a sizable group of Americans remain hesitant. A Pew Research Center survey in early March 2021 found that more than 30 percent of the public have no plans to get vaccinated. Democrats were more likely to have received, or to plan to get, a COVID-19 vaccine than Republicans, by a margin of 83 percent to 56 percent. Also, there are surprising numbers of holdouts among medical personnel and the military. In December 2020 Ohio governor Mike DeWine revealed that 60 percent of that state's nursing home workers had refused the vaccine. A mid-February report showed that two-thirds of enlisted people had turned down the vaccine during a nationwide campaign in the military. Such unexpected collisions between science and politics are playing a major part in the so-called vaccine wars in the United States and around the world.

## A Routine Part of Health Care

Vaccinations have long been a part of routine health care in the United States and most nations around the world. Schoolchildren receive shots to protect them from diseases such as measles, mumps, diphtheria, and whooping cough. Each year millions of Americans get vaccinated for seasonal flu. Vaccines developed for more serious diseases have been hailed as great scientific breakthroughs. In 1953 Jonas Salk, a medical researcher at the University of Pittsburgh, announced that he had developed a vaccine for polio, a virus that can cause paralysis in those it infects. The threat it posed for children made its eradication a political priority. Salk's vaccine proved to be safe and effective in large clinical trials that were the first of their kind. Rushed into production, it was soon being injected into the arms of millions of children worldwide.

Salk never patented his discovery. Today, however, vaccines can generate large profits for multinational pharmaceutical firms. The drug companies that developed vaccines for COVID-19 had invested large sums on prior research and declared they would not profit on vaccine sales. Yet they are not doing the work for free. "They would never make the drug and make a loss," says Anton Hutter, a patent attorney and biochemist. "It's harsh to say [but] these big drug companies are in it for the money."[2]

> "[Pharmaceutical companies] would never make the drug and make a loss. It's harsh to say [but] these big drug companies are in it for the money."[2]
>
> —Anton Hutter, a patent attorney and biochemist

## Challenges of Testing and Distribution

The race to develop an effective vaccine for COVID-19 brought new attention to the political agreements and partnerships that aid the drug industry. Pfizer relied on German funding for its research and development, while Moderna received most of its financial support from the United States. But both companies made use of US government guarantees to purchase their vaccines if they received FDA approval, thus reducing the financial risk. In fact, using new technologies, these firms were able to create vaccines for the coronavirus with extraordinary speed. But developing a vaccine is only part of the challenge that drug companies and health care officials face in trying to quell a pandemic like COVID-19. And each further step, from testing to distribution, presents its own political hurdles.

Testing a new vaccine usually takes several years. Merck's human papillomavirus (HPV) vaccine Gardasil went through nine years of testing before it won FDA approval. However, with COVID-19 threatening to lay waste to lives and economies the

*A patient receives a vaccination to protect him from COVID-19. Vaccines to protect people from serious diseases have been hailed as great scientific breakthroughs.*

world over, testing for vaccines was placed on a fast track. Critics warned that such haste was likely to weaken the usual safety standards. Others feared that too little testing would fail to uncover problems such as adverse effects on certain populations such as minorities and pregnant women.

Getting the vaccines into people's arms presents a whole new set of problems. Pointing to rollouts that initially were slow in many states, critics blasted the Trump administration's lack of a national plan. In addition, state and local health officials had to grapple with concerns about who should receive the vaccine first. Sometimes, efforts to follow protocols to the letter led to hundreds of doses of vaccine going to waste. Moreover, health officials had to overcome widespread misinformation about the vaccine. The speed of its development, combined with long-standing myths about the dangers of vaccination, left some people reluctant to get the shots.

"When our actions can have devastating consequences for people globally, near and far from us, then the moral obligation to protect everyone [with COVID-19 vaccines] is something we have to take very seriously."[3]

—Keisha Ray, a bioethicist at the University of Texas Health Science Center at Houston

Vaccines of all kinds have become one of the mainstays of health care in an interconnected world. Because they are so important, vaccines like those for COVID-19 are certain to attract controversy. "When our actions can have devastating consequences for people globally, near and far from us," says Keisha Ray, a bioethicist at the University of Texas Health Science Center at Houston, "then the moral obligation to protect everyone [with COVID-19 vaccines] is something we have to take very seriously."[3]

# CHAPTER ONE

# Developing the Vaccines

A lot can be accomplished in one weekend. On January 11, 2020, a Saturday, Chinese researchers published online the genetic sequence of the coronavirus that was spreading in Wuhan. Scientists at the Massachusetts-based biotech company Moderna seized on the release and got to work creating a vaccine. They were well prepared. Days earlier, Moderna's chief executive officer (CEO), Stéphane Bancel, had discussed the virus's deadly potential with Barney Graham, a researcher at the National Institutes of Health (NIH). They agreed that a vaccine could be a lifesaver and that every day mattered. They decided to work together to develop it. Inside the labs at Moderna and the NIH, scientists used cutting-edge technology to evaluate the Chinese map of the coronavirus and tailor a protective drug to its genetic blueprint. On Monday, January 13, two days after the Chinese release, the vaccine's gene sequence was done. The United States had yet to report its first official case of COVID-19, yet a vaccine to prevent its infection was essentially ready to be manufactured. A process that typically took years had been completed in forty-eight hours. When he announced his company's breakthrough, Bancel chose to downplay the challenge. As he explained to reporters, "This is not a complicated virus."[4]

## A Game-Changing Breakthrough

Developing a successful vaccine can be a game changer not only for public health but also for a company's bottom line. Prior to its breakthrough on the coronavirus, Moderna had not produced or sold a single commercial drug. The company's prospects were all based on an unproven technology. However, its vaccine announcement brought undreamed-of publicity and massive new interest from investors. With each positive report on clinical tests and manufacturing, Moderna's stock jumped higher. By December 2020 its market value had risen ninefold, to $67 billion.

The key to Moderna's rapid development of a COVID-19 vaccine was a technology called messenger RNA (mRNA). This genetic material controls how cells make proteins. Moderna's vaccine injects a tiny piece of mRNA from the coronavirus. This piece codes for the spike protein that enables the virus to latch on to healthy cells and invade them. Once the mRNA is injected, a person's immune system produces antibodies that target the viral spikes and neutralize the virus. Pfizer, a huge American pharmaceutical corporation, also used mRNA technology in its COVID-19 vaccine. Working with the small German company BioNTech, Pfizer began testing twenty vaccine candidates, whittling them down to four by April 2020.

Moderna, Pfizer, AstraZeneca, and other drug firms would have to negotiate a minefield of political and scientific challenges in their quest for a COVID-19 vaccine. The situation—trying to stop a deadly spreading virus in its tracks in real time—was unprecedented. Until now, developing vaccines for infectious diseases had always been a slow process of trial and error, one that took years—and often ended in failure. If an effective vaccine did emerge, it tended to arrive well after the worst of an outbreak had passed and death rates were already plummeting. Health experts note that practical public health measures like washing hands, disinfecting living and work areas, and getting basic medical treatment often do more to defeat infectious disease than vaccines or miracle cures.

Nonetheless, with the coronavirus's ability to spread unchecked, it became obvious that practical measures were not

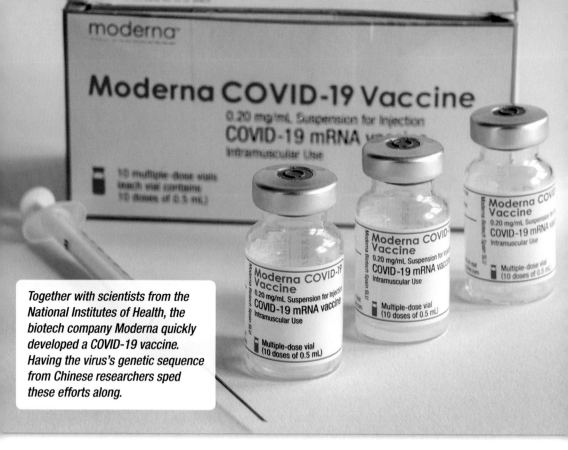

*Together with scientists from the National Institutes of Health, the biotech company Moderna quickly developed a COVID-19 vaccine. Having the virus's genetic sequence from Chinese researchers sped these efforts along.*

enough. As the death toll in America rose into the hundreds of thousands, most people regarded the rapid testing procedures and lightning rollouts for the vaccines as a necessary risk. Science and politics, not without some holdouts, converged to support the effort. David Wallace-Wells, a medical reporter for *New York* magazine, noted the irony that Moderna had already manufactured its vaccine and delivered it to the NIH for clinical trials when the first American COVID-19 death was made public. "This is—as the country and the world are rightly celebrating—the fastest timeline of development in the history of vaccines," Wallace-Wells wrote in early December 2020. "It also means that for the entire span of the pandemic in this country, which has already killed more than 250,000 Americans, we had the tools we needed to prevent it."[5] And the virus's grim business was far from over. By late March 2021, the total number of COVID-19 deaths in the United States had surpassed 545,000.

# A Postwar Success for the Mumps Vaccine

Prior to the COVID-19 vaccines, the fastest creation of a new vaccine was one for mumps, an illness that usually caused high fever and swollen salivary glands in children. In 1968 Maurice Hilleman, the top research scientist at pharmaceutical firm Merck, brought a mumps vaccine to market after only four years of development. As a less dangerous disease than polio or measles, mumps never produced a widespread panic in the United States. Many health officials downplayed its severity. A New York State Department of Health brochure in 1955 claimed, "Almost always a child is better off having mumps: the case is milder in childhood and gives him life-long immunity."[6] Yet mumps had presented a real threat to American soldiers since World War I. Only in the 1930s did scientists discover that mumps was caused by a virus. It was highly contagious, spreading easily in barracks during World War II, and causing disruptions in training and troop movements. A mumps infection often inflamed the testicles, bringing risk of permanent damage and infertility in teens and adults. Infection could also result in severe loss of hearing. Moreover, in America's post–World War II baby boom, a contagious disease that mainly struck children was bound to be a concern.

"This is—as the country and the world are rightly celebrating—the fastest timeline of development in the history of vaccines. It also means that for the entire span of the pandemic in this country . . . we had the tools we needed to prevent it."[5]

—David Wallace-Wells, a medical reporter for *New York* magazine

Hilleman based his mumps vaccine on an active strain of the virus. He got the strain from a throat swab of his daughter, Jeryl Lynn, whose mumps infection had given her a sore throat and swollen glands. In Merck's labs, Hilleman and his team attenuated the strain, or weakened it, by repeatedly running it through chicken embryos. This technique was pioneered by John Enders, a scientist who won the 1954 Nobel Prize for cultivating the polio virus. Vaccine with the weakened mumps strain did not cause a full-blown infection, but it was enough to trigger an immune response.

The breakthrough on a mumps vaccine helped promote widespread public acceptance of childhood vaccination. In 1971 Merck won Centers for Disease Control and Prevention (CDC) approval for Hilleman's combination of mumps vaccine with vaccines for measles and rubella. (Rubella, or the German measles, causes a distinctive red rash.) Required for school enrollment in many districts, the measles-mumps-rubella (MMR) vaccine became a quick and inexpensive tool to protect children from these diseases. Eventually, it became a fixture of public health worldwide.

## Seeking an AIDS Vaccine

Successes like the vaccines for polio and MMR strengthened the public's faith that medical research was on the road to eliminating most threats from contagious disease. But the appearance of acquired immunodeficiency syndrome (AIDS) in the early 1980s belied these hopes. AIDS was caused by the human immunodeficiency virus (HIV). The virus attacked the immune system of an otherwise healthy person, rendering it incapable of fighting off other infections. AIDS initially spread among gay males and intravenous drug users in the United States and Europe, causing some politicians and pundits to dismiss its impact on the wider society.

However, as the death toll rose, AIDS became the most politically charged disease in the United States before COVID-19. AIDS activists protested the lack of progress on a cure. In 1990 more than one thousand members of ACT UP, a radical gay activist group, stormed into the NIH to demand more participation in trials for a vaccine and other treatments. Their target was Dr. Anthony Fauci, then as now director of the NIH's National Institute of Allergy and Infectious Diseases (NIAID). Unbeknownst to the ACT UP protesters, Fauci actually was lobbying his colleagues for more input from gay activists.

During a visit to the National Institutes of Health in March 2020, President Donald Trump sought information about the research center's work with Moderna on a COVID-19 vaccine. Among the NIH scientists he met was one of the project's chief architects, Dr. Kizzmekia Corbett. The thirty-four-year-old doctor and immunologist explained how the vaccine could teach the body how to recognize the virus's spike protein and then fight to eliminate it. As Corbett later told *Nature* magazine, "If you want to go fast in a pandemic, then messenger RNA (mRNA) is a shoo-in. It can be manufactured very quickly in very vast quantities, and it's plug and play in that you can essentially just swap out the protein once you have the system down."

Corbett's own story is just as remarkable. She set her sights on a career in science at a young age. At the University of Maryland, Baltimore, she became a Meyerhoff Scholar, part of a program that develops women and minorities in science. Her meteoric rise at the NIH led to her lifesaving work on the mRNA vaccine. As an African American, she is also using her spare time—what there is of it—to keep the Black community informed about the vaccine's safety and effectiveness.

Quoted in Nidhi Subbaraman, "This COVID-Vaccine Designer Is Tackling Vaccine Hesitancy—in Churches and on Twitter," *Nature*, February 11, 2021. www.nature.com.

The protests helped fuel the federal effort to develop a vaccine. In 1997 President Bill Clinton promised that an AIDS vaccine would be created within a decade. Fauci's NIAID set up the Vaccine Research Center to focus on an AIDS vaccine. But scientists found that creating such a vaccine was a daunting task. The virus's extraordinary ability to mutate kept defeating potential vaccines. Trials not only failed but also proved risky to the test subjects. Despite the poor prospects, millions were spent on vaccine development each year. As Fauci recalls:

> Although some of us, myself included, were really less than cautiously optimistic, we were hoping that we would see some signal that would allow us to build on the next generation of a similar type of vaccine. . . . My job was to remind people that research is fundamentally a bunch of failures with an occasional bright light of a success and to tell them that we're not going to give up on vaccines.[7]

There is still no vaccine that will prevent HIV infection. Instead, researchers were able to develop a cocktail of drugs that effectively control the HIV virus in those already infected. For scientists and activists alike, the failed quest for an AIDS vaccine seemed to reveal the limits of modern medicine.

## A Partnership for Speed

Such perceived limits were bound to affect the push to develop a vaccine for COVID-19. To break through such limitations, it was necessary to go where no one had gone before—and in the process, get the public to buy in. This was the thought process that occurred to Peter Marks, the slender, bespectacled doctor in charge of regulating vaccine approval at the US Food and Drug Administration (FDA). A fan of the science-fiction series *Star Trek*, Marks had the perfect name for the laser-focused effort needed to produce a COVID-19 vaccine: Operation Warp Speed.

Marks's brainstorm was to bring together the Pentagon and the US Department of Health and Human Services (HHS) in a grand collaboration. They would use government expertise in science and logistics to support the pharmaceutical companies' efforts. The science end, including clinical trials, was led by Dr. Moncef Slaoui, who had years of research and development experience in the drug industry. Logistics, or strategies for manufacturing and distribution, were run by Gustave Perna, a four-star general. From the beginning, Operation Warp Speed proceeded like a battle plan. Housed in a suite at the HHS, Slaoui, Perna, and their lieutenants used as their model America's rapid buildup of the arms industry in World War II. Officers on board often showed up for meetings in uniform. Once Slaoui and his scientists decided to focus on three main types of vaccine—out of fifty candidates—the stage was set. An early memo established October 2020 as the target for a COVID-19 vaccine.

Inevitably, politics raced alongside the scientific push. In the spring, skyrocketing case rates and death tolls from COVID-19 in New York, New Jersey, and Massachusetts showed the virus's deadly potential. Lockdowns to stop the spread threatened to hobble what had been a strong economy. With the election only months away, Trump seemed to regard the coronavirus as the chief threat to his presidency. Publicly, at rallies jammed with cheering supporters, he began to tout the goal of having an effective vaccine by October, or end of the year at the latest. Privately, he urged government health officials and drug company executives to pick up the pace. Meanwhile, Trump's critics warned that his political meddling in the review process could endanger lives. They reminded people that vaccines, if not produced and vetted properly, could cause serious side effects, some even fatal. Reports circulated that even people on the inside were worried. White House aides scoffed at the doomsayers. "The rapid research, development, trials and eventual distribution of a Covid-19 vaccine is emblematic of President Trump's highest priority: the health and safety of the American people," said White House spokesperson Judd Deere. "It has nothing to do with politics."[8]

Yet politics found its way into every aspect of the COVID-19 vaccine story. Some even criticized the name Operation Warp Speed. They said it played into anti-vaccination fears that the vaccine would be rushed and potentially dangerous. Even Fauci, the Trump administration's leading expert on the coronavirus, expressed displeasure with the name. "I'm a little concerned by that name," he said, "because it can imply by warp speed that you're going so fast that you're skipping over important steps and are not paying enough attention to safety, which is absolutely not the case."[9] Fauci's experience with failures related to an AIDS vaccine left him cautious overall. Along with scientists outside the administration, he continued to voice doubts that a COVID-19 vaccine could be produced by the end of the year. Some experts claimed that even at "warp speed" an effective vaccine could take years to develop. But many ordinary Americans, having lost loved ones or been separated from them for months, welcomed the intense campaign to break the pandemic.

## Rejecting and Embracing COVAX

As American-based drug companies raced to develop a vaccine for the United States, global health groups sought ways to vaccinate poorer nations. Leading these efforts was the World Health Organization (WHO), along with the vaccine alliance Gavi and the Coalition for Epidemic Preparedness Innovations. The WHO's initiative, called COVAX, had signed up 172 nations to pool resources in quest of COVID-19 vaccines. Under COVAX, pharma-

# A Rushed Deployment for Vaccines in China

Authoritarian nations ruled by a single party can often steamroll over political issues regarding vaccine safety. In the spring of 2020, Chinese scientists had already engineered COVID-19 vaccines and begun large-scale clinical trials. Yet even while the trials were ongoing, the Chinese Communist Party (CCP) enabled favored groups in China to get injections. Tens of thousands of doses went to health care personnel, drug company workers, and government officials. In Beijing alone, ten thousand residents received the vaccine candidate from the Chinese firm Sinovac.

There was also the question of consent. The CCP sought to immunize the most essential workers first—staff at state-owned companies, teachers, supermarket employees, and others. Such people doubtless felt pressured to line up for the shots to meet the national emergency. Biotech experts worried that the party's haste might backfire. However, phase 3 trial results, released in January 2021, were positive. The Chinese vaccine was 78 percent effective in preventing symptomatic coronavirus cases. "I feel more relieved now that I have protection," says Ethan Zhang, who waited in line four hours to get his shot in the eastern city of Yiwu. "Since they've started using it on some people on an emergency-use basis, it shows that there's a certain guarantee."

Quoted in Sui-Lee Wee and Elsie Chen, "Vaccine Unproven? No Problem in China, Where People Scramble for Shots," *New York Times*, January 7, 2021. www.nytimes.com.

ceutical companies and universities produced nine potential vaccines. Each vaccine had to be proved safe and effective in each individual country before it was distributed. Vaccinations prioritized health care workers, then the elderly and those with serious health conditions. Doses for the ninety-two poorest countries in the program are paid for by wealthy nations. In September 2020 the WHO set a goal of delivering 2 billion vaccines worldwide.

At first, there were two notable holdouts from COVAX: the United States and China. China decided to join the WHO's vaccine program only in October 2020. Analysts noted that, having apparently suppressed COVID-19 at home, the Chinese government could use "vaccine diplomacy" to spread its influence among less fortunate nations. China encouraged several client states, including countries in South America, to accept its own Chinese-made vaccine.

As for the United States, its withdrawal from the WHO began in July 2020, after Trump criticized the group's handling of the early coronavirus outbreak in Wuhan. In Trump's view, the WHO had soft-peddled China's failure to alert the world when the virus first began to spread. Moreover, in line with his America First policies, Trump focused on providing COVID-19 vaccines to Americans. Mike Pompeo, Trump's secretary of state, stressed America's commitment to also deliver vaccines around the world but kept this effort separate from COVAX and the WHO. The Trump administration's position drew fire from globalist critics, like California representative and physician Ami Bera. "Joining Covax is a simple measure to guarantee U.S. access to a vaccine—no matter who develops it first," said Bera on September 2, 2020. "This go-it-alone approach leaves America at risk of not getting a vaccine."[10]

When Joe Biden took office as president, he reversed course and announced that the United States would join COVAX. He

Upon taking office, President Joe Biden announced that the United States would join COVAX, an initiative by the World Health Organization (WHO) with the goal of delivering 2 billion vaccines worldwide.

also authorized payment of more than $200 million in membership fees to the WHO. In February 2021 Biden pledged $4 billion to COVAX programs, with $2 billion going immediately to the Vaccine Alliance, a public-private health partnership for global immunization. Nonetheless, COVAX officials said they still had only enough doses to cover 3.3 percent of the population in participating nations.

> "I'm a true believer that people, they don't really know their limits. And usually, they have the tendency to underestimate what they can produce."[11]
>
> —Albert Bourla, CEO of Pfizer

With advances in genetics and computer analysis, developing vaccines has become a much speedier process than in the past. Whereas vaccines once took years or even decades to create, COVID-19 vaccines have been produced in a matter of months. Prior vaccines like the one for mumps in the 1960s helped build public confidence in immunization programs. But failures like the fruitless search for an AIDS vaccine also pointed to the limitations of modern medicine. With Operation Warp Speed and the societal threat of COVID-19, vaccines have entered a new era of political controversy, but also one of hope and progress. "I'm a true believer that people, they don't really know their limits," says Pfizer CEO Albert Bourla. "And usually, they have the tendency to underestimate what they can produce."[11]

# Testing the Vaccines

On August 25, 2020, Moderna CEO Stéphane Bancel received a disheartening phone call. At the time, Bancel's upstart biotech company was in the midst of a high-profile race to get the first vaccine for COVID-19 approved in America. Initial results of clinical tests looked good. Moderna seemed in position not only to secure FDA approval for its vaccine ahead of schedule but also to beat its much larger competitors, including Pfizer, to the finish line. But Moncef Slaoui, head of Operation Warp Speed, had some bad news for Bancel. Moderna's final stage of testing had to be delayed. According to FDA officials, Bancel's company had failed to enlist enough minority candidates in its trials for the vaccine.

News reports had repeatedly stressed that Blacks and Hispanics were especially vulnerable to the coronavirus. Thus, it was vital that Moderna establish its vaccine's effectiveness for these groups. In addition, widespread racial unrest over the summer months had heightened tensions. George Floyd's May 25 death while in police custody in Minneapolis left raw nerves regarding unfair treatment of African Americans. At the same time, recruiting more minority candidates would take Moderna at least one to three weeks, almost ensuring that the Pfizer-BioNTech vaccine would be first in line for approval. Bancel was disappointed, but he also understood both the science and the politics of the situation. "I would rather we have higher diverse participants and take one extra week," Bancel told CNBC.

"We believe we could have one of the best vaccines. We want to ensure we have data for all the people who could benefit and be protected."[12]

## From Preliminary Tests to Human Trials

Urgency worldwide due to mounting death tolls changed almost everything about the development of a COVID-19 vaccine, including human trials. The testing process for vaccines is typically complex and rigorous, with many layers of trials and review. Since vaccines are aimed not at people who are already sick but at large populations of healthy individuals, the issue of safety is all the more essential. To ensure that standards of safety and effectiveness are met, the testing process alone often takes several years. "We have to remember that the fastest we've ever seen this really being done is four years," said Dr. David Shulkin, former president and CEO of Beth Israel Medical Center in New York City. "The traditional methods and processes for developing vaccines take a great deal of time."[13] In the minds of many, however, including doctors, scientists, and politicians, the coronavirus's threat to public health ruled out the luxury of such a lengthy process. "If you want every 't' crossed and 'i' dotted, how many more people will die or suffer from COVID-19?" asked Dr. Walt Orenstein, a professor of medicine at Emory University and former director of the National Immunization Program. "It's not an easy decision, it is a breakneck speed for moving things."[14]

"I would rather we have higher diverse participants and take one extra week. We believe we could have one of the best vaccines. We want to ensure we have data for all the people who could benefit and be protected."[12]

—Stéphane Bancel, CEO of the biotech firm Moderna

Vaccine development typically begins with a discovery stage. In this step, researchers study a virus's structure and its ability to attack the body. Once they decide on the most promising kind of vaccine to pursue, they proceed to create it in the lab. Then scientists conduct preclinical tests to study the vaccine's effects on animals. If the results are positive, the vaccine can be tested on people in clinical trials. These trials, in three phases, are subject to extremely tight regulation by the FDA.

Phase 1 of clinical trials usually tests the vaccine on less than one hundred people. Researchers primarily look for safety concerns, as well as information about best dosage and serious side effects that might outweigh the benefits. Phase 2 conducts a larger study on a few hundred subjects, again with an emphasis on safety and side effects. Phase 3 represents the gold standard of vaccine clinical trials. Thousands of test subjects are randomly divided into two groups—those who receive the vaccine and those who receive a placebo, or some other control medication. Subjects are carefully chosen to represent the larger population's breakdown by age, gender, race, and ethnicity. FDA scientists and outside experts who study the results strive to ensure that the vaccine is safe and works as designed. Even after a vaccine is approved and delivered for large populations, scientists continue to monitor it for safety and side effects.

A participant in the clinical trial of the Moderna COVID-19 vaccine has his temperature checked. Moderna's final stage of testing had to be temporarily delayed because it had failed to enlist enough minority candidates in its trials for the vaccine.

## Speeding Up the Review Process

Significantly, the three phases of vaccine testing are usually separated by one to two years. This allows time for detailed statistical analyses and, if necessary, changes in the next phase of trials. Here is where Operation Warp Speed departed from the usual protocols. The FDA and other regulatory bodies made the COVID-19 vaccine their top priority. To speed up the review process, all the phases of the clinical trials were planned at once to eliminate any delays. The trials were allowed to overlap in some cases. FDA scientists worked tirelessly to evaluate each phase. And when they found safety concerns, they halted the process for further study and only restarted it when the question was resolved. The pharmaceutical firms also submitted the trials to extra scrutiny. For example, in September 2020 the drug company AstraZeneca suspended its Phase 3 COVID-19 vaccine trials in the United States when one of its volunteers developed a serious neurological problem. The company conducted a thorough safety review before resuming the trials. Dr. Francis Collins, director of the NIH, told a Senate hearing on vaccine testing that AstraZeneca's prompt response should inspire public confidence in the process.

Despite such assurances, many experts remained skeptical that safety standards could be maintained when there was so much emphasis being placed on rapid evaluation. Some worried that serious side effects, which can take weeks or months to appear in test subjects, might be missed. The risk to otherwise healthy members of the public, they warned, should not be minimized. "It is possible to have a vaccine by the fall or winter," said Dr. Greg Poland, director of the Vaccine Research Group at the Mayo Clinic in Rochester, Minnesota. "It is not possible to have a vaccine by fall or winter that has gone through the usual safety testing. Speed is a tradeoff with safety."[15]

> "It is possible to have a [COVID] vaccine by the fall or winter. It is not possible to have a vaccine by fall or winter that has gone through the usual safety testing. Speed is a tradeoff with safety."[15]
>
> —Dr. Greg Poland, director of the Vaccine Research Group at the Mayo Clinic

In 1976 the CDC's rush to procure a vaccine for swine flu raised important questions that are still relevant today. Drug companies worried about being sued if fast-tracked clinical trials failed to predict serious side effects. The drugmakers sought government protections in case of lawsuits, but Congress refused to provide those protections.

Forty-four years later, the officials behind Operation Warp Speed had to deal with similar concerns. In this case, HHS secretary Alex Azar invoked a 2005 law that provides legal protection to firms like Pfizer and Moderna that make or distribute crucial medical supplies, including vaccines. Only so-called willful misconduct by the companies falls outside the legal shield. Under the obscure law, federal protection against lawsuits over injuries or adverse effects lasts until 2024. According to Rogge Dunn, a Dallas labor and employment attorney, it was the drastically reduced timeline for clinical trials that caused Azar to employ this unusual legal shield. "It is very rare for a blanket immunity law to be passed," said Dunn. "Pharmaceutical companies typically aren't offered much liability protection under the law."

Quoted in MacKenzie Sigalos, "You Can't Sue Pfizer or Moderna If You Have Severe Covid Vaccine Side Effects. The Government Likely Won't Compensate You for Damages Either," CNBC, December 17, 2020. www.cnbc.com.

## Controversy over the Swine Flu Vaccine

Skipping steps in developing a vaccine can result in colossal failures that endanger lives. Health experts skeptical about going too fast in quest of a coronavirus vaccine could point to a near tragedy that unfolded in 1976. In February of that year, David Lewis, a nineteen-year-old private at Fort Dix in New Jersey, died from a mysterious flu. When several more soldiers contracted the virus, the CDC conducted blood tests. The virus proved to be closely related to the so-called Spanish flu of 1918, which had killed 675,000 Americans and more than 50 million others worldwide. News reports trumpeted the possible return of one of history's deadliest pathogens.

At the time, medical experts noted that conditions for fighting such an outbreak had improved considerably since World War I. Unlike in 1918, when the flu-causing virus had yet to be identified, scientists now had the means to create a vaccine for such a dangerous flu. And even though no other cases had been found outside Fort Dix, the CDC decided on an unprecedented plan. CDC director David Sencer, citing a government projection that an outbreak of swine flu in the fall could kill more than 1 million Americans, advised that everyone in the United States be vaccinated.

The swine flu controversy, like COVID-19, emerged in a presidential election year. President Gerald Ford already found himself in a precarious political state. Ford had not been elected to the presidency, but instead, as vice president, had replaced Richard Nixon when Nixon resigned in 1974. Placing additional pressure on Ford was a memo written by Sencer. In it the CDC head stated that the administration could handle unnecessary health expenditures better than preventable deaths and illness. As one of Ford's aides said later, "There was no way to go back on Sencer's memo. If we tried to do that, it would leak. That memo's a gun to our head."[16]

On March 24 Ford approved the plan for mass vaccination. In a national speech, he admitted that no one could predict how serious the outbreak might be, but he could not take a chance with

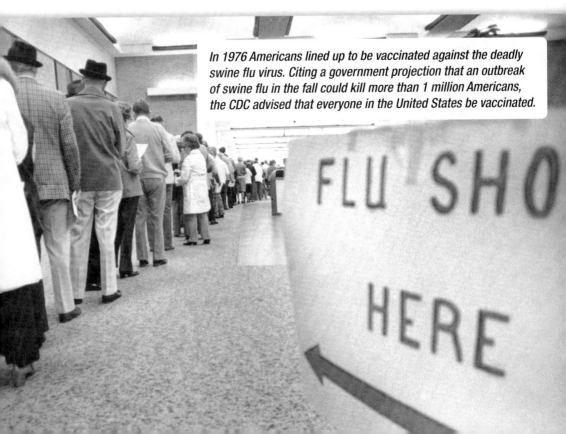

*In 1976 Americans lined up to be vaccinated against the deadly swine flu virus. Citing a government projection that an outbreak of swine flu in the fall could kill more than 1 million Americans, the CDC advised that everyone in the United States be vaccinated.*

FLU SHO

HERE

the health of Americans. Drug companies rushed volunteers into clinical trials, then rolled out a swine flu vaccine within months. By October people began to get shots. However, Ford's critics noted that Lewis was still the only fatality due to the swine flu and that the disease apparently had not spread beyond Fort Dix. Ford was accused of fearmongering during an election year. Moreover, news reports began to question the vaccine's safety. Three people in Pittsburgh supposedly died from heart attacks after receiving the dose. Dozens more came down with Guillain-Barré syndrome, a rare nerve disorder resulting in muscle weakness and paralysis. Public outcry led the government to cancel the vaccination program. More than 45 million people had received a vaccine that largely went untested. In November Ford lost the election to Georgia governor Jimmy Carter. In addition, millions of Americans lost faith in the public health system for years. Labeling the whole episode a fiasco, the *New York Times* warned, "The danger now is that the whole idea of preventive medicine may be discredited."[17]

## Case Numbers and Vaccine Development

Unlike swine flu, certain coronaviruses before COVID-19 did loom as a legitimate threat. A viral disease called severe acute respiratory syndrome (SARS) first appeared in China in 2003. WHO doctors issued a global alert, noting an unusual pneumonia that spread among hospital workers. However, after killing 770 people across China, the virus nearly died out, with only four small subsequent outbreaks. In 2012 another coronavirus-based disease, called Middle East respiratory syndrome (MERS), arose in Saudi Arabia. Once more, the disease seemed lethal, showing an alarming death rate among those infected of 35 percent. But like SARS, MERS proved to be less infectious than originally feared and did not spread widely.

Scientists hoped to use the SARS and MERS outbreaks to develop a vaccine against coronaviruses. However, the relatively low infection rate for both diseases stymied their efforts. As cas-

In raw numbers, Brazil trails only the United States in its death toll from COVID-19. Gaining access to an effective vaccine has thus become a major priority for the people of Brazil. But on November 9, 2020, the Brazilian government halted a Phase 3 trial of a promising Chinese vaccine after a trial volunteer died. President Jair Bolsonaro, a COVID-19 skeptic, hailed the suspension as a political victory. Earlier, Bolsonaro had criticized China's handling of the coronavirus outbreak in Wuhan. He also had questioned the effectiveness of the Chinese company Sinovac's vaccine, which was undergoing clinical trials in Brazil under the authority of the national health institute. In October 2020, Bolsonaro had squelched a health institute plan to buy 46 million doses of the Sinovac drug.

The episode shows the political minefield that vaccine candidates must negotiate in many countries. National health officials in Brazil insisted the Sinovac trial suspension was unnecessary and arose mainly because of politics. Police reports treated the trial participant's death as a probable suicide and unrelated to the vaccine's safety. João Doria, governor of São Paulo and Bolsonaro's chief rival, saw the trial's delay as a political ploy, and he attacked the president for endangering the lives of Brazilians.

es diminished, research funding—and interest—also dwindled. A team of Texas scientists who had created a vaccine to address the deadly coronavirus strains was among those affected. By 2016 the team was ready to test the vaccine on humans, but their quest for funding met with indifference from the government and the drug industry. "We tried like heck to see if we could get investors or grants to move this into the clinic," said Dr. Peter Hotez, codirector of the Center for Vaccine Development at Texas Children's Hospital. "But we just could not generate much interest. We could have had this ready to go and been testing the vaccine's efficacy at the start of this new [COVID] outbreak in China."[18] Without a large and identifiable threat, the team's research remained stuck in the lab.

COVID-19's deadly potential led to the opposite effect. When the virus became a public concern in the early months of 2020, some scientists pushed radical plans to speed up research on a lifesaving vaccine. In late March an article in the *Journal of Infec-*

*tious Diseases* suggested that volunteers should be infected with COVID-19 in order to test vaccines more rapidly. The proposal drew surprising support. Thirty-five members of Congress wrote to the FDA and HHS urging them to green-light the plan. Websites sprang up to enlist volunteers. Proponents of the plan noted that the coronavirus presented much less of a threat to young, healthy people. Skeptics in the medical community, however, dismissed the idea as too reckless to even consider. With no treatment available for the disease, a trial volunteer whose infection developed into serious illness could face a death sentence. "We don't yet know why some people get sick and others don't," said Christine Grady, chief of the department of bioethics at the NIH Clinical Center. "It makes an assessment that it's OK to subject a certain age group to risk a little bit too fast for me."[19]

> "We don't yet know why some people get sick and others don't. . . . It makes an assessment that it's OK to subject a certain age group to risk a little bit too fast for me."[19]
>
> —Christine Grady, chief of the department of bioethics at the NIH Clinical Center

In the end, the proposal was abandoned in favor of traditional clinical trials in the United States. But other nations embraced the idea. In February 2021 scientists at Imperial College London announced a government-funded plan to infect ninety otherwise healthy young adults with COVID-19 to test their immune response to vaccines and treatments. Each volunteer was due to receive about $6,200 for participating in the yearlong study.

## Politics and Science on a Collision Course

Throughout the summer months of 2020, balancing risk and recklessness was also on the minds of journalists and medical experts in America. Many criticized Trump's promise, in his speech for the Republican National Convention in August, to produce a COVID-19 vaccine by the end of the year, if not sooner. An NBC News fact-check disputed Trump's claims: "There is also no evidence that an effective vaccine will be delivered by the end of the year. There are four vaccines currently in clinical trials in the U.S., with the one from Moderna furthest along. But it's impossible to know if these vaccines will prove effective."[20] Experts such as Orenstein warned that a lot of things could go wrong and that producing an effective vaccine so quickly would take a miracle. Many researchers had similar reservations.

Others, however, pointed out that Trump's pledge was not so outlandish, since the vaccine trials were actually based on a longer-term effort. "This looks like it was developed overnight in one year, but in actual fact people have been working on this for the better part of a decade," said Dr. Gabor Kelen, chair of the department of emergency medicine at Johns Hopkins University.

*Speaking before the Republican National Convention in August 2020, President Trump promised that the United States would produce a COVID-19 vaccine by the end of the year.*

"There just hasn't been a good pandemic to be able to do the kind of trials to show how effective it is with very low rates of side effects."[21]

At any rate, as the presidential campaign moved into the home stretch, politics and science continued on a collision course. Pfizer vaccine researchers, who had originally predicted that a vaccine could not be ready until mid-2021 at best, now had a much rosier outlook. Behind the scenes, Albert Bourla, the company's CEO, had constantly pushed his people to meet aggressive goals. He sought vaccine approval by October, along with 100 million doses available by year's end. At the same time, Bourla kept his distance from Trump's own optimistic rhetoric. He insisted that company decisions on the vaccine must be free of politics.

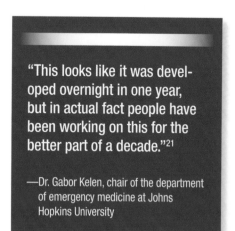

"This looks like it was developed overnight in one year, but in actual fact people have been working on this for the better part of a decade."[21]

—Dr. Gabor Kelen, chair of the department of emergency medicine at Johns Hopkins University

## An Extraordinary Success

Nonetheless, in such a hothouse atmosphere, Bourla's every move was bound to be scrutinized. In October, as Moderna paused its Phase 3 trials to add more minority subjects, Pfizer suddenly found itself leading the field. The company could have released a preliminary analysis in October based on thirty-two cases of COVID-19 infection (divided between those who got the vaccine and those who received a placebo). However, after consulting with FDA officials, Pfizer decided to wait for an increase in the case count. On November 7, four days after the election, Bourla released the FDA's analysis of the clinical trials. The Pfizer-BioNTech vaccine proved to be 95 percent effective in protecting against COVID-19 infection. Not long afterward, Moderna's trials achieved similar results. The path-breaking vaccines had gone far beyond the expectations of most health experts.

Trump and his supporters questioned the timing of the Pfizer release. Some noted that Pfizer issued its press release without even notifying the Trump administration about the results. But others simply focused on the extraordinary success of this public-private collaboration. It was a triumph of scientific know-how and political will. Graham T. Allison, professor of government at Harvard University, stressed two main causes for the rapid development of a COVID-19 vaccine:

> The first was the capitalist system, which facilitated competition between private, profit-seeking biotech and pharmaceutical companies to produce a lifesaving product. . . . Second is Operation Warp Speed. Had Mr. Trump not created the initiative, appointed as its leader a man who knows the vaccine development world, and given him license to spend $10 billion outside normal contracting procedures, Covid-19 vaccines would still be only works in progress.[22]

Clinical trials for vaccines must avoid not only scientific stumbling blocks but also political minefields. Moderna found this to be true when the FDA delayed its COVID-19 trials in order to enlist more minority subjects. Hasty development and testing of vaccines can have disastrous results, as with the rushed rollout of the swine flu vaccine. Nonetheless, the public-private partnership that led to successful trials for a COVID-19 vaccine promises to boost public confidence in health care research.

# CHAPTER THREE

# Producing and Distributing the Vaccines

Rare indeed in today's government is the mea culpa, or accepting personal responsibility for an error. Thus, Americans might have been shocked to hear one of the top two officials running Operation Warp Speed admit to a major mistake. On December 19, 2020, four-star army general Gustave Perna, head of logistics for the program, admitted he failed to communicate clearly with states about early shipments of the Pfizer-BioNTech vaccine. Perna's original forecasts proved to be mistaken because he underestimated the time and steps needed to clear shipments of vaccine for release. Due to the confusion, the second wave of shipments included far fewer doses than governors in more than a dozen states had expected. Instead of a smooth rollout, health officials had to deal with bottlenecks and delays. "I want to assure everybody, and I want to take personal responsibility for the miscommunication," Perna told Capitol Hill reporters. "I know that's not done much these days, but I am responsible. . . . There is a delay between what is available and what is releasable, because we're talking about hundreds and thousands and millions of doses that we want to make sure are right."[23]

Perna's press conference drew the usual praise and blame from the usual sources. But his admission also highlighted the stiff logistical challenges facing government at every level. In the race to get huge quantities of vaccine manufactured and shipped to every corner of the nation, scientists, politicians, health officials, and business leaders had to pool their efforts as never before.

## Getting Vaccine from the Freezer into Arms

For the American public, concerns about the details of getting immunized gave way to delight at the clinical trials' success. The trial results led promptly to the FDA granting emergency-use approval for both the Pfizer and Moderna vaccines in December 2020. Many Americans, finally seeing light at the end of the COVID-19 tunnel, assumed distribution plans would now fall into place. But like almost everything else related to the COVID-19 vaccine saga, the scale and complexity of the

When the initial rollout of the Pfizer-BioNTech COVID-19 vaccine did not go smoothly, US Army general Gustave Perna, one of the officials in charge of Operation Warp Speed, took personal responsibility for the problems.

enterprise threatened to delay the rollout. As health reporter Julie Wernau noted:

> Delivering Covid-19 shots to sites around the country is just the first step in vaccinating the population. Getting them from the freezer and into arms is another journey, complicated by the special handling the doses require but also because of cumbersome data-management systems. Sites must take precautions to ensure that they don't contribute to the spread of the virus, measures that can slow down administration of shots. And at many locations, demand for doses has outstripped supply.[24]

> "Delivering Covid-19 shots to sites around the country is just the first step in vaccinating the population. Getting them from the freezer and into arms is another journey. . . . And at many locations, demand for doses has outstripped supply."[24]
>
> —Julie Wernau, health reporter

With public interest running high, news reports dwelt on how the two major vaccines were alike and different in production, storage, and delivery. The Pfizer vaccine required storage at -94°F (-70°C), while the Moderna version was stored at -4°F (-20°C). Once thawed in special refrigerators, both vaccines had to be used within six hours. Health care workers had to constantly monitor the thawing times at vaccination sites. Each Pfizer dose contained 30 micrograms of vaccine, compared to 100 in the Moderna shot. Pfizer's plan called for a priming dose followed by a booster shot twenty-one days later. Moderna set a period of twenty-eight days between its first and second doses.

On February 27, 2021, the FDA authorized emergency use for a third COVID-19 vaccine, this one created by the drug company Johnson & Johnson. The Johnson & Johnson vaccine proved to be 85 percent effective in preventing severe disease, and it required only one dose. Although Twitter and Facebook users

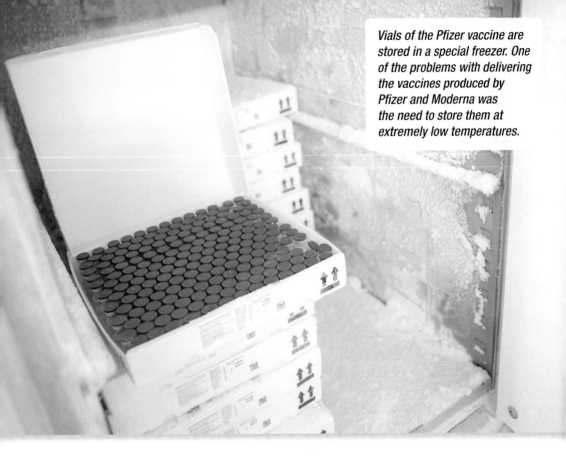

*Vials of the Pfizer vaccine are stored in a special freezer. One of the problems with delivering the vaccines produced by Pfizer and Moderna was the need to store them at extremely low temperatures.*

debated the three vaccines' pros and cons, it made little difference overall. Health officials noted that, with supplies scarce in the early rollout, people were not likely to have a choice about which vaccine they received.

More pressing were the thornier issues of who should be vaccinated first and how to get the vaccine distributed equitably to the most vulnerable populations. Some questioned whether rich nations that produced the vaccines should give them first to their own people. Many scientists insisted that the vaccination effort had to be global in order to be ethical. Medical experts and ethicists had been debating these matters since the coronavirus first appeared. Inevitably, science and politics would both play a role in the process. "What's interesting about this, is this is one of the few times in human history where everyone on the planet has actually been affected by the same set of circumstances," said Laurie Zoloth, professor of religion and ethics at the University of

In an effort to immunize the largest possible groups with preexisting health conditions, Washington, DC, offered early doses to people who are overweight. Medical experts warned that the plan could slow distribution to segments of the DC population, including the aged, that desperately needed the first shots available. At a DC council meeting in January 2021, Health Director LaQuandra Nesbitt defended the plan. She hoped it would help get rapid vaccinations to people who faced the worst outcomes from coronavirus infection. These included residents of impoverished, mostly Black wards in DC, with high rates of obesity and related health problems.

Adding these adults to the initial rollout led to an organizational nightmare, with those in charge of the district's website and phone lines for registration scrambling to cope. "When you have something [like obesity] that's that common, it becomes a question of social policy implementation," says David Kass, a cardiology professor at Johns Hopkins University. "It's almost too common—it would be very hard, I think." Nonetheless, a March 2021 study from the CDC tended to support the district's plan. It found that 78 percent of Americans who were hospitalized or died from COVID-19 were overweight or obese.

Quoted in Julie Zauzmer, "All Overweight D.C. Residents Will Get Priority for the Coronavirus Vaccine. Experts Are Skeptical," *Washington Post*, January 21, 2021. www.washingtonpost.com.

Chicago. "And it's an extraordinary moment for humans to figure out, what do we do now?"[25]

## Vaccinating 6 Million People in a Month

The rush to vaccinate huge numbers of people to avert disaster is not without precedent. In 1947 New York City health officials faced just such a crisis. On March 1, 1947, an American business traveler named Eugene Le Bar felt feverish as he checked into a hotel in midtown Manhattan along with his wife. The Le Bars were already weary following a long bus ride from Mexico City. Eugene, suffering from neck pain and a pounding headache, went straight to bed. Four days later, he checked into Bellevue Hospital with a temperature of 105°F (40.6°C) and a maddening rash on his face and hands. Transferred to a clinic for contagious disease,

Le Bar continued to decline. Doctors were puzzled by his ailment. Still undiagnosed, Eugene died on May 10.

Within days, other patients at the clinic began to display symptoms like Le Bar's. Test samples sent to the US Army Medical School Laboratory revealed the horrible truth: the patients had smallpox. Hugely contagious and often fatal, smallpox had already killed hundreds of millions worldwide since the turn of the century. But cases had not arisen in New York since before World War II. Health officials soon traced the outbreak to Le Bar and his trip to Mexico.

"What's interesting about this, is this is one of the few times in human history where everyone on the planet has actually been affected by the same set of circumstances. And it's an extraordinary moment for humans to figure out, what do we do now?"[25]

—Laurie Zoloth, professor of religion and ethics at the University of Chicago

Israel Weinstein, New York City's health commissioner, faced a dilemma. Nearly all New Yorkers had received a shot for smallpox as children. Yet the vaccine was not foolproof. In some people it did not offer full protection, while in others the immunity could fade. Le Bar himself had a vaccination mark on his arm. Weinstein decided the only solution was to vaccinate the city's entire population as quickly as possible.

To implement his plan, Weinstein had to walk a political tightrope. At press conferences and on the radio, he tried to convey the seriousness of the situation without sparking panic. There was also the possibility of bad reactions to the vaccine, including encephalitis, or inflammation of the brain. However, Weinstein did not waver. After rapidly using up the city's stockpile of vaccine, he worked with Mayor William O'Dwyer to secure additional doses from naval depots, military bases, and private manufacturers. Soon New Yorkers all over the city were waiting in long lines to get their shots. The rollout proceeded with few impediments. Within a month, 6 million New Yorkers were vaccinated for smallpox. In the end, with Weinstein's guidance, the city avoided a potential catastrophe. "The first thing he did was level with the public," says

Dr. David Oshinsky, director of the Division of Medical Humanities at New York University's School of Medicine. "He told them that smallpox had arrived in the city, and that it was possible there was going to be a spread—and that it was an extremely communicable and dangerous disease. And he said, 'We will provide enough vials of vaccine to effectively protect the city.'"[26]

## Curtailing the Asian Flu

Rapid vaccine distribution helped corral another deadly outbreak in 1957. In April of that year, virologist Maurice Hilleman read about a mysterious flu rampaging through Hong Kong. The disease had struck more than 10 percent of the city's inhabitants, including many school-age children. Hilleman realized at once that a potential pandemic was in the works. Through his connections at the Walter Reed Army Medical Research Institute in Washington, DC, he was able to obtain samples of the virus from Hong Kong. Tests showed that the virus differed from known flu strains. Hilleman wasted no time, asking six different pharmaceutical companies to create a vaccine using his samples. Since regulatory standards of the time were much less strict, the vaccine was approved for immediate use.

Doses arrived just in time for the predicted fall outbreak. The deputy surgeon general warned that 10 to 20 percent of Americans could become infected. Priority for the first flu shots went to police, firefighters, medical workers, and other frontline personnel. President Dwight D. Eisenhower received one of the first shots to encourage the populace to get on board. By mid-November, with more than 40 million doses administered, the pandemic showed signs of easing. Some politicians and state health officials dismissed the nationwide vaccination effort as an overreaction to a mild virus. But the CDC estimates that 116,000 Americans and 1.1 million worldwide died from the 1957 flu. Hilleman believed the numbers in America could have been much worse. Years later, he told an interviewer, "That's the only time we ever averted a pandemic with a vaccine."[27]

Once out of the freezer and thawed for use, the Pfizer and Moderna COVID-19 vaccines are on the clock. If not dispensed within a certain period, the doses must be tossed out. This fact has led to late-night drugstore shoppers or people on the street getting a sudden opportunity to be vaccinated at the last minute. That some of these people may be too young or too healthy to be eligible yet for the vaccine rankles some sticklers. A doctor in Houston was fired for giving leftover doses to his wife and relatives. But health officials say the main thing is to ensure that the precious vaccine does not go to waste.

A new online service called Dr. B is helping meet this goal. It enables people to sign up to receive any extra doses left over at vaccination sites. Users must provide their name, date of birth, and other information such as their cell phone number so they can be notified by text message. Each person must be prepared to travel to a given site within fifteen minutes of notification. According to Brooke Williams, a Black chorus singer in New York and one of Dr. B's earliest clients, "Hearing about shots that were getting thrown out was just heartbreaking and infuriating."

Quoted in Katie Thomas, "Hunting for a Leftover Vaccine? This Site Will Match You with a Clinic," *New York Times*, March 9, 2021. www.nytimes.com.

## Debates over Priority for Vaccination

In 1957 nearly everyone agreed that frontline medical workers and first responders should be among the first to receive vaccinations. Even before the COVID-19 vaccine began shipping, there was near-universal agreement that the same rules should apply in the current pandemic. Nonetheless, there were still debates about who should get priority for vaccination. Most people assumed the elderly, as being most vulnerable to the coronavirus, should receive priority. Death rates showed that Americans over age sixty-five were up to seventy-three times more likely to die of COVID-19 than those in their twenties. Yet a significant number of scientists and statisticians had other ideas. They pointed to studies that showed the best way to deploy a vaccine that is highly effective, like the ones for COVID-19, is to first vaccinate people who are most apt to spread the virus. That meant healthy young people, including young adults and college students, who generally have more social interaction on a daily basis.

Ultimately, however, most states chose to follow the recommendations of the CDC. They first immunized health care personnel and residents of long-term care facilities. Then they concentrated on frontline essential workers (police, firefighters, and workers in agriculture, grocery stores, manufacturing, and the US Postal Service) and people aged seventy-five and older. Next in line were people aged sixty-five to seventy-four and those younger than sixty-four with serious health conditions that could increase the severity of COVID-19 infection.

The debate was complicated further by questions of equity. Research showed that African Americans and Hispanics were dying from the coronavirus at significantly higher rates than White Americans. Black Americans were about twice as likely to die from COVID-19 than White Americans. This was partly due to greater percentages of Blacks working in essential jobs with more face-to-face contact. Moreover, minority communities tended to live with extended family, had fewer options for health care, and often experienced longer wait times for testing and treatment. "If I were in charge," says Kirsten Bibbins-Domingo, an epidemiologist and expert in health disparities, "I would want to actively monitor the demographics of who is getting vaccinated—to make sure the groups disproportionately affected are actually the ones receiving the vaccines. And if they're not, I'd want to work with the civic leaders in those communities to figure out how we could do this better."[28]

> "If I were in charge, I would want to actively monitor the demographics of who is getting vaccinated—to make sure the groups disproportionately affected are actually the ones receiving the vaccines."[28]
>
> —Kirsten Bibbins-Domingo, an epidemiologist and expert in health disparities

## Varying Success in the Vaccine Rollouts

The Trump administration urged state and local governments to create their own plans for distributing the vaccine. However, as

UPS and FedEx trucks fanned out across the nation to deliver the first shipments, many state health departments were still unprepared. Critics remained skeptical that the vaccination program could succeed without strict federal oversight. They noted that the vaccine was being allocated by the number of adults in each state, instead of by age and high-risk health problems. They also feared that the initial limits on vaccine supply would expose some medical workers and nursing home residents to weeks of unnecessary coronavirus risk. Some local health officials deplored what they saw as a lack of federal coordination and funding. Dr. Jeffrey Duchin, a Seattle doctor with the National Association of County and City Health Officials, said local health departments desperately needed more financial support for such a huge effort.

States varied widely in the pace of their early rollouts. Some smaller states achieved remarkable success getting shots into arms. West Virginia rejected a federal program to enlist the CVS and Walgreens pharmacy chains for vaccinating nursing homes,

*A nurse in West Virginia records information from a vaccine recipient at a drive-through site. West Virginia was particularly successful in getting the state's allotment of vaccines into the arms of its citizens.*

9

an option it deemed too slow. Instead, the state turned to a network of 250 local pharmacies. Most of these already had accounts with longtime patients, which helped ease scheduling and paperwork. The state also recruited the National Guard to deliver vaccines to long-term care facilities and health clinics. "We are a scrappy state that's resilient," says Dr. Clay Marsh, West Virginia's chief coronavirus official and vice president of health services at West Virginia University. "But we absolutely rely on the creativity and the innovation of all of our people. Because we don't want to rely on external resource requirements for us to be able to do what we need to do."[29] By the end of January 2021, the state had already used 85 percent of the doses it had received, placing it behind only North Dakota.

By contrast, populous states like California, New York, and Georgia struggled out of the gate. Vaccinations proceeded at a snail's pace as state officials set confusing guidelines about who was eligible for doses. Some delays were due to shortages of vaccine and uncertain supply lines from the manufacturers. In the first seventeen days of the rollout, only 1 percent of New York City's residents received shots. City health officials canceled thousands of appointments to balance out shortages, instead of ensuring that available doses made their way into people's arms. Workers at vaccination sites were forbidden to contact community groups in order to deliver more shots. Over one weekend in late January 2021, thousands of doses sat inside freezers as New Yorkers frantically sought appointments. "We're still not good at allowing people on the ground to improvise, if that's what it takes to get shots in arms," said Mark Levine, chair of the New York City Council's health committee. "This is a war in which we can't lose a single day, and good for the staff who was ready to do that work. But I think we need to

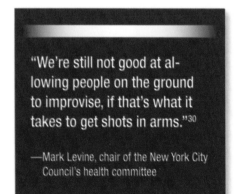

"We're still not good at allowing people on the ground to improvise, if that's what it takes to get shots in arms."[30]

—Mark Levine, chair of the New York City Council's health committee explicitly empower them to do that. Unfortunately, that didn't appear to happen today."[30]

Distributing the coronavirus vaccines has proved to be a contentious program politically. The initial rollout featured delays, skewed communications, and wrangling over who deserved priority to receive shots. The race to vaccinate large populations was reminiscent of similar efforts to immunize New York City for smallpox in 1947 and the entire United States for the 1957 Asian flu. Despite the uneven performance of some states in the COVID-19 vaccine effort, overall America's results were among the world's best. By March 10, 2021, the United States had delivered more than 93 million doses of vaccine, more than any other nation. Percentage-wise, the US had vaccinated 18 percent of its population, and Great Britain 33 percent. By contrast, the European Union, with its reliance on layers of bureaucracy, had managed to inoculate only 6.5 percent of its people.

# CHAPTER FOUR

# Promoting the Safety of the Vaccines

On January 31, 2021, a sunny Saturday, thousands of people drove to Dodger Stadium in Los Angeles to get their appointed shots of COVID-19 vaccine. The stadium vaccination site is one of the largest in America, servicing as many as eight thousand recipients in a day. At the time, Los Angeles County was vaccinating those age sixty-five and older, plus health care workers and nursing home staff and residents. However, on this day, anti-vaccine protesters at the front gates threatened to derail the process. They waved American flags and signs claiming that the vaccines were dangerous and the coronavirus itself was a scam. Some shouted at drivers who were lining up in their cars. One protester was dressed as the grim reaper.

Notified about the protests in advance, Los Angeles police shut down the site at two o'clock in the afternoon, got the protesters to leave the premises, and reopened the site an hour later. No appointments were missed, and apparently no vaccine was wasted. But the disruption and chaos demonstrated how the anti-vaccine movement could affect the rollout. State and local officials condemned the extremists who sought to intimidate people who were trying to get vaccinated. With more than three hundred people in Los Angeles County dying each day from the virus, there was no time for misguided protests. "Unbelievable," tweeted

Los Angeles City Council president Nury Martinez. "If you don't want the vaccine fine, but there are millions of Angelenos that do. 16,000 of your neighbors have died, so get out of the way."[31]

## A Variety of Vaccine Skeptics

Anti-vaccine protests go back decades—indeed, even centuries. Each time government health officials pursue a widespread vaccination program, some people suspect the worst. They may claim that the drug actually causes the disease it is supposed to protect against. They might insist that the true purpose of a vaccine is hidden and malign, ranging from the implantation of tiny microchips to sterilizing people by chemical means. And, as experts admit, concerns about vaccines are not completely unfounded. Some vaccines have led, in rare cases, to serious side effects. That is why clinical trials typically take years of study before a panel of experts will recommend approval. At any rate, doctors note that a person is far more likely to be felled by an infectious disease than a dose of vaccine.

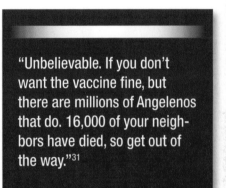

"Unbelievable. If you don't want the vaccine fine, but there are millions of Angelenos that do. 16,000 of your neighbors have died, so get out of the way."[31]

—Nury Martinez, Los Angeles City Council president

The speed with which the COVID-19 vaccines have been developed and tested has also raised flags about safety. Skeptics include not only anti-vaccine diehards but also people who are usually comfortable with vaccination. For some, the name Operation Warp Speed signified recklessness, not urgency. But their hesitance to get the shots is likely to disappear once large segments of the population have been immunized with no ill effects.

According to Gallup polls, willingness to get vaccinated for COVID-19 sank to a low of 50 percent in September 2020 but has been rising ever since. By late December the number had climbed to 65 percent. In February, polling revealed that 71 percent were willing, the highest percentage yet. "This makes sense,"

An anti-mask and anti-vaccine protester shares his views at a "freedom rally" in New York City. The speed with which COVID-19 vaccines have been developed has caused some individuals to be skeptical about their safety.

says John Brownstein, an epidemiologist at Boston Children's Hospital. "As these vaccines have more time on the market, you personally know people that have had it, and that social network will lend itself to creating a snowball effect of more people willing to get the vaccine."[32]

## The Politics of Trusting the Vaccines

Nonetheless, poll numbers revealed that a substantial group still resisted the vaccine push. Observers say some of that resistance may be due to America's deep political divisions. Donald Trump, one of the most polarizing presidents in memory, hardly inspired confidence in those who bitterly opposed his administration. Trump and his team publicly prodded FDA officials to accelerate the vaccine approval process, leading some to conclude that safety guidelines were being fudged or ignored. However, to allay such fears, the CEOs of Pfizer and Moderna signed assurances that their clinical trials would not skimp on necessary safeguards. And FDA officials dismissed suggestions they were influenced by pressure from the White House. "Science and data guided the FDA's decision," said FDA chief Stephen Hahn. "We worked quickly because of the urgency of this pandemic, not because of any other external pressure."[33]

Some holdouts, including minorities, may have been influenced by political wrangling. During the 2020 presidential campaign, there were plenty of hints that the COVID-19 vaccines might be rushed and unsafe. In a September speech in Wilmington, Delaware, then-candidate Joe Biden said, "Let me be clear: I trust vaccines. I trust scientists. But I don't trust Donald Trump, and at this moment, the American people can't either."[34] During the presidential debates, Biden suggested that a safe and effective vaccine could not be produced before mid-2021. In the debate between candidates for vice president, Kamala Harris said she would be first in line for a vaccine backed by scientists, but not one touted by Trump. Then-vice president Mike Pence accused Harris of undermining public confidence in the coming vaccines.

> "As these vaccines have more time on the market, you personally know people that have had it, and that social network will lend itself to creating a snowball effect of more people willing to get the vaccine."[32]
>
> —John Brownstein, an epidemiologist at Boston Children's Hospital

## The Anti-Vaccine Crusade

Beginning in the 1980s, the crusade against vaccines was propelled mostly by celebrities and nonmedical pseudo-experts. In 1982 a reporter named Lea Thompson caused a sensation with a documentary titled *DPT: Vaccine Roulette*. The program alleged that the DPT vaccine for diphtheria, pertussis (or whooping cough), and tetanus presented a number of health threats to children, including sudden infant death syndrome. Thompson's documentary also led to many lawsuits against the vaccine's

## Reluctance Among Health Care Professionals

Reluctance to get the COVID-19 vaccine appears in a surprising group: health care workers. A January 2021 survey by Surgo Ventures, a nonprofit organization that focuses on health and social problems, found that significant numbers of doctors, nurses, and medical support staff had turned down the Pfizer and Moderna vaccines. Reasons for the rejection ranged from concerns about safety or effectiveness to worries about the speed of the vaccines' development. Of the more than twenty-five hundred American health care workers in the survey, 53 percent had been offered the vaccine, and 15 percent of those had declined the offer. Many of the two hundred respondents who had refused the shots claimed that there was a lack of evidence that the vaccine worked to prevent coronavirus infection. Some preferred to let others go first in order to ensure the vaccine's safety. A few had friends who had experienced unpleasant reactions to the shots.

Despite its small size, the survey raised troubling questions for the vaccination effort nationwide. According to Hannah Kemp, director of programs for Surgo Ventures, "If health care workers are hesitant and we need to take specific efforts to overcome that, we are going to have a huge challenge in convincing the general population to take the vaccine in the U.S."

Quoted in Megan Cerullo, "Many Health Care Workers Are Refusing to Get a Covid-19 Vaccine," CBS News, January 19, 2021. www.cbsnews.com.

manufacturer, as well as formation of the anti-vaccine group Distraught Parents Together.

In the 1990s popular daytime talk shows invited anti-vaccine authors and celebrities to air their views, with little pushback from experts. Even more influential was a 1998 study by British physician Andrew Wakefield, linking the MMR vaccine to neurological problems in children, including autism. Wakefield's research was later shown to be fraudulent, and his medical license was revoked. Yet his autism claims persist to this day, repeated endlessly by anti-vaccine activists, including many celebrities. Vaccine alarmists went on to suggest that many other vaccines also increased the childhood risk of autism. Celebrities who questioned the safety of vaccines included Jenny McCarthy, Matt Lauer, Robert De Niro, Jessica Biel, and Robert F. Kennedy Jr.

In the past decade, social media has provided anti-vaccine voices with a vast new platform. Activists often pressure parents to refuse vaccinations for their children. For example, an online group called Stop Mandatory Vaccination influenced a Colorado mother named Geneva Montoya to avoid getting flu shots for her family. Her four-year-old son later became seriously ill with the flu, experiencing high fever and a seizure. Nonetheless, group members posting on Facebook also convinced Montoya to reject a

Celebrities, such as actress Jessica Biel, questioned the safety of vaccines in general.

doctor's prescription for an antiviral medicine. Instead, they recommended so-called natural cures such as lavender herbs and peppermint oil. Montoya's son ended up dying from his flu infection. Moreover, her ten-month-old baby barely recovered after his heart stopped from the flu.

The 178,000 members of Stop Mandatory Vaccination troll social media, spreading misinformation about the supposed dangers of vaccines. Due to such groups, a disease like the measles, thought to be eliminated in 2000, is resurging. Experts also worry that a third of millennials, under the influence of social media, now oppose vaccination. A July 2020 report from the Center for Countering Digital Hate found that the following for anti-vaccine social media accounts had increased by 7.8 million people since 2019. Wendy Sue Swanson, a pediatrician at Seattle Children's Hospital, has met with Facebook officials to discuss all the misleading posts about vaccines. "You wouldn't go see a pediatrician who doesn't hold medical certification, but on the Internet, you might listen to them," says Swanson. "Facebook isn't responsible for changing quacks, but they do have an opportunity to change the way information is served up."[35]

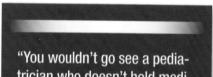

"You wouldn't go see a pediatrician who doesn't hold medical certification, but on the Internet, you might listen to them. Facebook isn't responsible for changing quacks, but they do have an opportunity to change the way information is served up."[35]

—Wendy Sue Swanson, a pediatrician at Seattle Children's Hospital

## Fighting Against Bogus Anti-Vaccine Information

Fake social media posts triggered an outbreak of panic about the COVID-19 vaccine. In December 2020, as the first vaccine doses were rolling out, users shared a Facebook screenshot claiming that a nurse in Alabama had fainted just after receiving her shot and had been found dead shortly thereafter. The post spread widely before it could be decisively proved false. Officials

In an orange grove in Hemet, California, Luz Gallegos polled farmworkers on who intended to get the COVID-19 vaccine. Not one hand was raised. Gallegos, who leads a team of Latino health care activists, says they have found the same reluctance all across the state. Some of the workers repeat widespread stories about the vaccine, including the belief that each dose features a microchip enabling the government to track and deport undocumented workers. Many get their information from posts on Facebook and other social media platforms.

As essential workers, agricultural workers in California have been prioritized for early vaccination. Experts warn that their participation is essential to ending the pandemic. Working long hours in close quarters can subject the workers to greater risk of viral spread. Gallegos and her team hope that hesitancy about the vaccine will fade as workers see their friends and relatives get shots without bad consequences. Access to facts, not myths, should help. "No one had come here to explain anything [about the vaccine]," says Ezequiel Chavez, a farmworker in Ontario, California, "at least not anyone who really knows anything about it."

Quoted in Rolfe Winkler and Daniela Hernandez, "Advocates Fight Covid-19 Vaccine Concerns Among Agricultural Workers," *Wall Street Journal*, March 9, 2021. www.wsj.com.

at the Alabama Department of Public Health hurried to contact all state hospitals that had administered the vaccine. They were able to confirm that no one receiving the shot had died. Officials then issued a statement denying the fake reports. But the rebuttal by the health department took time and effort better spent elsewhere.

Disinformation like the story about the Alabama nurse can often outpace efforts to stop it. To counter the onslaught, health care workers are forming online campaigns of their own to get the truth out. They recruit vaccine advocates to monitor hashtags and keywords related to the COVID-19 vaccine. When anti-vaccine forces try to spread false reports like the Alabama nurse story, the health care networks flood social media sites with detailed corrections and messages in support of the vaccines. A group called Shots Heard Round the World has enlisted nine hundred volunteers globally, many of them physicians, to respond to anti-vaccine attacks in real time. The group maintains a website where health care workers can report instances of anti-vaccine propaganda. Doctors and nurses who contribute to the fight can put their own reputations and careers at risk. Anti-vaccine mobs sometimes take revenge by bombarding rating sites like Yelp with negative reviews of physicians.

Sunny Jha, an anesthesiologist in Houston, Texas, has created a Twitter campaign called #ThisIsOurShot to share health care workers' experiences with getting the vaccine. He admits the battle against the anti-vaccine crowd can get ugly. "It's turning into a military campaign, in terms of how we have to treat the opposition," says Jha. "As a new group we had to kind of be smart about how exactly we strategize."[36]

## Promoting Vaccine Safety for Minorities

For minorities in the United States, the fight against anti-vaccine misinformation is especially crucial. According to the CDC, African Americans and Hispanics are dying from the coronavirus at three times the rate of Whites and are three times more likely to require hospitalization. For Native Americans, the risk of hospitalization from COVID-19 is four times greater than for Whites. Yet studies show that more than half of Blacks and Latinos are hesitant about getting vaccinated for COVID-19. A survey by the National Foundation for Infectious Diseases found that nearly one-third of African Americans refuse to get the shots. Experts stress the need to build trust in minority communities in order to accomplish a more equitable distribution of the vaccine. Early in the rollout, vaccination rates trailed death rates from the coronavirus for both Blacks and Hispanics in most states.

There are many reasons why minority communities are hesitant to get the vaccine. The speed with which it was developed and tested has not inspired trust in its safety. Blacks have told pollsters that they are worried about their health insurance paying for the vaccine, even though vaccination is free for everyone. Minority neighborhoods tend to have fewer facilities for getting the vaccine and poorer health outcomes in general.

A Navajo woman cries as she talks about COVID's devastating effects on her family. For Native Americans, the risk of hospitalization from COVID is four times greater than for Whites.

In addition, there are troubling historical episodes that still resonate with people of color. Many point to the infamous experiments at the Tuskegee Institute in Macon County, Alabama, from 1932 to 1972. The studies, conducted on six hundred African American males without their knowledge or consent, tracked the progression of untreated syphilis over a long period. Many of the men died or suffered terrible health problems. The Tuskegee incident and other examples of poor medical treatment for Blacks have left a legacy of skepticism.

To build trust among minorities, some African American doctors are actively promoting the safety of the COVID-19 vaccines. The National Medical Association (NMA), a professional group for Black doctors, seeks to relieve fears among Blacks and other minorities about bad outcomes from vaccination. When the vaccines first won approval, the NMA reviewed the data and gave the FDA's emergency authorization its endorsement. To increase vaccination rates for minorities, the NMA has set up meetings and webinars with church groups, universities, and neighborhood organizations. Its goal is to puncture myths about the vaccine in order to ease long-standing anxieties. As Gabrielle Perry, a clinical epidemiologist in New Orleans, Louisiana, explains, "Medical professionals have to understand that the fear of Covid-19, which is this invisible looming foe, that fear does not always outweigh the very clear and well-documented danger of going to a health care system that has proven itself to be as deadly as disease."[37]

> "Medical professionals have to understand that the fear of Covid-19 . . . does not always outweigh the very clear and well-documented danger of going to a health care system that has proven itself to be as deadly as disease."[37]
>
> —Gabrielle Perry, a clinical epidemiologist in New Orleans

In the race to vaccinate Americans for the coronavirus, health officials have had to confront anti-vaccine protests and counter myths about the vaccine. Many protesters are part of a decades-long movement to discredit lifesaving vaccines and sow doubt about their safety. To counter the anti-vaccine message online, doctors, medical workers, and concerned citizens have joined together to replace misinformation with facts. This work is vital to the success of the vaccine, especially for the most vulnerable communities in America.

# SOURCE NOTES

## Introduction: Fighting Fear and Skepticism

1. Quoted in Dan Diamond, "'We Want to Be Educated, Not Indoctrinated,' Say Trump Voters Wary of Covid Shots," *Washington Post*, March 15, 2021. www.washingtonpost.com.
2. Quoted in Chris Stokel-Walker, "Have COVID-19 Vaccines Changed Intellectual Property for Good?," Raconteur, January 26, 2021. www.raconteur.net.
3. Quoted in Sigal Samuel, "How a Black Bioethicist Makes the Case for Vaccination to People of Color," Vox, February 16, 2021. www.vox.com.

## Chapter One: Developing the Vaccines

4. Quoted in Sharon LaFraniere et al., "Politics, Science and the Remarkable Race for a Coronavirus Vaccine," *New York Times*, November 21, 2020. www.nytimes.com.
5. David Wallace-Wells, "We Had the Vaccine the Whole Time," *New York*, December 7, 2020. www.nymag.com.
6. Quoted in Elena Conis, "An Excerpt from *Vaccine Nation: America's Changing Relationship with Immunization*," University of Chicago Press Books. https://press.uchicago.edu.
7. Quoted in *IAVI Report*, "A Living History of AIDS Vaccine Research," March-April 2009. www.vaxreport.org.
8. Quoted in Sharon LaFraniere et al., "Scientists Worry About Political Influence over Coronavirus Vaccine Project," *New York Times*, August 20, 2020. www.nytimes.com.
9. Quoted in Nathaniel Weixel, "Some Worry 'Operation Warp Speed' Plays Into Anti-vaccination Movement's Hands," *The Hill* (Washington, DC), May 31, 2020. www.thehill.com.
10. Quoted in Conor Finnegan, "US Declines to Join Global COVID-19 Vaccine Effort Because of WHO's Role," *Science*, November 25, 2020. www.sciencemag.org.
11. Quoted in Jared S. Hopkins, "How Pfizer Delivered a Covid Vaccine in Record Time: Crazy Deadlines, a Pushy CEO," *Wall Street Journal*, December 11, 2020. www.wsj.com.

## Chapter Two: Testing the Vaccines

12. Quoted in Meg Tirrell and Leanne Miller, "Moderna Slows Coronavirus Vaccine Trial Enrollment to Ensure Minority Representation," CNBC, September 4, 2020. www.cnbc.

13. Quoted in Dennis Thompson, "A COVID-19 Vaccine by Fall Is Possible, but at What Cost?," WebMD, May 11, 2020. www.webmd.com.

14. Quoted in Robert Kuznia, "The Timetable for a Coronavirus Vaccine Is 18 Months. Experts Say That's Risky," CNN, April 1, 2020. www.cnn.com.

15. Quoted in Thompson, "A COVID-19 Vaccine by Fall Is Possible, but at What Cost?"

16. Quoted in Christopher Klein, "When the US Government Tried to Fast-Track a Flu Vaccine," History, September 2, 2020. www.history.com.

17. Quoted in Richard Fisher, "The Fiasco of the 1976 'Swine Flu Affair,'" BBC, September 21, 2020. www.bbc.com.

18. Quoted in Mike Hixenbaugh, "Scientists Were Close to a Coronavirus Vaccine Years Ago. Then the Money Dried Up," NBC News, March 5, 2020. www.nbcnews.com.

19. Quoted in Helen Branswell, "Infect Volunteers with Covid-19 in the Name of Research? A Proposal Lays Bare a Minefield of Issues," Stat, May 1, 2020. www.statnews.com.

20. Jane C. Timm and Jane Weaver, "Fact Check: No Evidence for Trump's COVID-19 Vaccine Claim," NBC News, August 27, 2020. www.nbcnews.com.

21. Quoted in Christopher White, "Some Experts Said Trump Would Need a 'Miracle' to Develop a Vaccine in Less than a Year," Fox 45 News, December 14, 2020. www.foxbaltimore.com.

22. Graham T. Allison, "Who Made the Vaccine Possible? Not WHO," *Wall Street Journal*, December 24, 2020. www.wsj.com.

## Chapter Three: Producing and Distributing the Vaccines

23. Quoted in Isaac Stanley-Becker et al., "'I Am Responsible': Warp Speed Chief Accepts Blame for Reduced Vaccine Doses but Creates New Confusion About Quality Control Steps," *Washington Post*, December 19, 2020. www.washingtonpost.com.

24. Julie Wernau, "Why Administering Covid-19 Vaccine Is So Hard," *Wall Street Journal*, February 14, 2021. www.wsj.com.

25. Quoted in UChicago News, "The Ethics of COVID-19 Vaccine Distribution, with Laurie Zoloth (Ep. 63)," *Big Brains* (podcast). https://news.uchicago.edu.
26. Quoted in John Florio and Ouisie Shapiro, "How New York City Vaccinated 6 Million People in Less than a Month," *New York Times*, December 18, 2020. www.nytimes.com.
27. Quoted in Lina Zeldovich, "How America Brought the 1957 Influenza Pandemic to a Halt," JSTOR Daily, April 7, 2020. https://daily.jstor.org.
28. Quoted in Sigal Samuel, "Should People of Color Get Access to the Covid-19 Vaccine Before Others?," Vox, October 28, 2020. www.vox.com.
29. Quoted in Laura Strickler and Lisa Cavazuti, "'We Crushed It': How Did West Virginia Become a National Leader in Covid Vaccination?," NBC News, January 31, 2021. www.nbcnews.com.
30. Quoted in Kevin T. Dugan, "'I Vaccinated 3 People': NYC Stopped Workers from Giving Out More Shots," *New York*, January 31, 2021. www.nymag.com.

## Chapter Four: Promoting the Safety of the Vaccines

31. Quoted in Olivia Niland, "Anti-vaxxers Temporarily Shut Down One of the Largest COVID-19 Vaccination Sites in the US," BuzzFeed News, January 31, 2021. www.buzzfeednews.com.
32. Quoted in Nicholas Nissen, "Americans' Willingness to Get COVID-19 Vaccines Reaches Record High: Poll," ABC News, February 10, 2021. www.abcnews.go.com.
33. Quoted in Matthew Perrone et al., "States Will Start Getting COVID-19 Vaccine Monday, US Says," Associated Press, December 14, 2020. www.apnews.com.
34. Quoted in Sydney Ember, "Biden, Seizing on Worries of a Rushed Vaccine, Warns Trump Can't Be Trusted," *New York Times*, September 16, 2020. www.nytimes.com.
35. Quoted in Taylor Telford, "Anti-vaxxers Are Spreading Conspiracy Theories on Facebook, and the Company Is Struggling to Stop Them," *Washington Post*, February 13, 2019. www.washingtonpost.com.
36. Quoted in Mohana Ravindranath, "Doctors Bring the Fight to Anti-vaxxers Online," Politico, February 15, 2021. www.politico.com.
37. Quoted in Eric Boodman, "With Painstaking Effort, Black Doctors' Group Takes Aim at Covid-19 Vaccine Hesitancy," Stat, January 22, 2021. www.statnews.com.

## Books

Arthur Allen, *Vaccine: The Controversial Story of Medicine's Greatest Lifesaver*. New York: W.W. Norton, 2008.

Peter J. Hotez, *Preventing the Next Pandemic: Vaccine Diplomacy in a Time of Anti-Science*. Baltimore: Johns Hopkins University Press, 2021.

Paul Offit, *Deadly Choices: How the Anti-vaccine Movement Threatens Us All*. Philadelphia: Basic Books, 2015.

Meredith Wadman, *Science, Politics, and the Human Costs of Defeating Disease*. New York: Penguin, 2018.

Brett Wilcox, *Jabbed: How the Vaccine Industry, Medical Establishment, and Government Stick It to You and Your Family*. New York: Skyhorse, 2018.

## Internet Sources

Richard Fisher, "The Fiasco of the 1976 'Swine Flu Affair,'" BBC, September 21, 2020. www.bbc.com.

John Florio and Ouisie Shapiro, "How New York City Vaccinated 6 Million People in Less than a Month," *New York Times*, December 18, 2020. www.nytimes.com.

Sharon LaFraniere et al., "Politics, Science and the Remarkable Race for a Coronavirus Vaccine," *New York Times*, November 21, 2020. www.nytimes.com.

Taylor Telford, "Anti-vaxxers Are Spreading Conspiracy Theories on Facebook, and the Company Is Struggling to Stop Them," *Washington Post*, February 13, 2019. www.washingtonpost.com.

Julie Wernau, "Why Administering Covid-19 Vaccines Is So Hard," *Wall Street Journal*, February 14, 2021. www.wsj.com.

# Websites

### Centers for Disease Control and Prevention (CDC)

www.cdc.gov

The CDC works around the clock to protect America from health, safety, and security threats, both foreign and in the United States. The CDC website contains abundant information on vaccines, including sections on safety, immunization for children, storage of vaccines, and correcting vaccine misconceptions.

### History

www.history.com

The History website provides an excellent source of information on world history. It includes a variety of articles about the history of vaccines, including those for smallpox, polio, whooping cough, and other diseases. There are also articles about the politics of vaccines, such as "Can the Government Make Vaccines Mandatory?"

### The History of Vaccines

www.historyofvaccines.org

The History of Vaccines is a website that explores the role of immunization in society and examines its continuing contributions to public health. The website contains a timeline of vaccine history, articles on how various vaccines were developed and tested, and features about how political considerations can fuel or derail the creation of vaccines.

### US Food and Drug Administration (FDA)

www.fda.gov

The FDA helps protect the public health by ensuring the safety, efficacy, and security of drugs, biological products, medical devices, and more. The FDA's website contains valuable information about the process for testing and approving vaccines, including the recent COVID-19 versions. The section on how the FDA operates according to laws and regulations shows the intersection of science and politics.

# INDEX

*Note: Boldface page numbers indicate illustrations.*

# PICTURE CREDITS

# ABOUT THE AUTHOR

John Allen is a writer who lives in Oklahoma City.